THE DREAMER

By Lady Tiffany

the Dreamer
Copyright © 2019 Lady Tiffany
Artwork © 2019 Lady Tiffany

ISBN: 9781798152324

Published by N-Spired Productions & Services LLC
Edison, New Jersey
908.372.0203
NSpiredProductions@live.com

Printed in the United States of America. All rights reserved under International Copyright Law and may not be reproduced in whole or in part in any form without expressed written consent from the Publisher.

"A winner is a dreamer who never gives up."

–Nelson Mandela

Dedicated to...

*my first Love and all you dreamer's out there.
Be and stay encouraged through
the good, bad, and ugly because
love conquers and heals.*

Contents

The Dreamer 1

Soldier's Heart 5

Yesterday 7

What It's All About 9

Beauty Is 13

I hate / I love 15

Sunlight 17

Finding My Way 18

A Love So True 21

Just Be 25

Farewell Party 29

Heaven On Earth 32

I Know What It's Like 35

As If Loneliness Were My Friend 39

A Gift To Myself 41

Good Heart.. 45

Clarity... 47

Love Worthy 49

I Move On 51

My Loneliness 55

Sober Mind 57

Origin Of Wisdom 59

Action Speaks 61

The Truth... 62

THE DREAMER

You may call me a dreamer

So, what if it is true?

My dreams gave me peace of mind

when there was none to find

My dreams have seen me through

    heartaches

        hopeless moments of despair

        stood by my side

        when no one else cared

My dreams have lent me breath

    when I was too weak to take one on my own

Oh, how my dreams have now matured and grown!

I'm proud of my dreams, cause they belong to me, and me alone

So close to my heart, pressed against my soul, showing me the light of my faith, so I can gain control of my destiny as I stroll down this illusion of reality

My dreams don't invite the company of pain, suffering, self-pity or fear, my dreams are always near

My dreams have their own

    Soul

        Spirit and

            Heartbeat

My dreams are so very gentle

My dreams keep me going on

    inspiring me to create and sing my

    life's love songs

I nurture them with my deeds as I plant

    crops of love seeds

        one by one

            and day by day

                they come to life

My dreams are truly the best part of me!

So, call me a dreamer

        for it is true

            and

        I'm so happy to share

            my dreams with you

SOLDIER'S HEART

So much has happened in such a little time

I can't tell what's real, fake, or really mine

I cry dry tears that never seem to fall

My heart's the fool that risked it all

Yes, I'm blessed for my heart is a soldier

    so strong

    yet tender

so, I will always remember

    the bitter sweetness of love

    the joy that the battle brings

for oh such beautiful songs love inspired me to sing

A soldier's heart
      is what I carry
           within it knows
                  when to cry or bleed

My soldier's heart guides me in all scenes of
      life and love, to bring peace through to
      me and to all who choose to embrace
      the tenderness of my vulnerabilities

My heart will grow the strength to battle
      love again so I can love me, being my
      own best friend

YESTERDAY

Today's pain is tomorrow's lesson

Today's confusion is tomorrow's growth

Today's tears are tomorrow's wisdom

Today's fear is tomorrow's strength

Today's heartache is tomorrow's joy

for yesterday was sure a hell of a day!

No Judgement Self-Reflection Zone

WHAT IT'S ALL ABOUT

It's not about me

It's not about you

      but about the deeds of love we do

how we devote our time

how we create and cherish our peace of
      mind

how we share our souls to assist in another
      person's life to build relationships

      that will grow and last

It's about working

      hard and letting go of the past

It's about moving

      forward into darkness so you can find the light within

It's about starting

      even when you don't know

      where to begin

No, it's not about you

It's not about me

      but about the sun in the sky

      the home of birds that fly

      the vast ocean that roars

      and our ancestors buried beneath

      the ancient sea's floor

See, we must start to realize that life is a
      ride of moments and we can choose to
      build or destroy

So, will the earth be your playground or your
      toy? For this message is for all ages of
      men
            women
                  girls
                        and boys
                            who have a
                        positive vision and a
                        plan to take a stand

And if you so agree
      sign on this unity
      line_____

BEAUTY IS

Beauty can never fade within for it is much
      deeper than the surface of the skin

Despite one's own features
      we are all God's creatures

The Spirit lives deep in one's soul
      where beauty is knowing love
      so intimately you become whole

Beauty is not just a face or body

it's much more than what you can see

beauty lives in you and me

For beauty is love unmasked

shining through your soul

touching another wholeheartedly

Beauty is the best of you and me

yes, everything sweet, gentle, and kind

beauty is a state of mind

Once you get to know the love that lives
    within you

it will shine through

yes, believe this your beauty to be true

beauty lives inside of you

I HATE / I LOVE

I hate the fact that I love you

>even when it appears to feel so good
>something isn't right with my soul

Being in love is supposed to bring rest not

>sleepless nights

>with useless fights

Wondering if it is right, or just a wannabe in

>a "sinsuationship" that leads to the
>emptiness longing for true love even
>more

I know it makes no sense logically that I
      would hand you the weapon of my
      trust

I believed it was love but it was just lust
      pureness of connection to what is
      higher than hate

Love is beyond practical or emotional
      reasons, learning to let go of past
      times embracing new seasons.

Honestly, I hate
      yes, I hate not to love
      for my soul knows love rules the world

SUNLIGHT

The sun shines

The sun shines on me

In me the sun shines

The sun shines into the heaviness and darkness of my soul

    light penetrating darkness

    leaving no deliberating soul, heart or mind, to be

My soul in a moment connects by a sincere confession from a heart that can now see divine truth

Don't you want to be free?

Don't you?

FINDING MY WAY

Don't just sit there crying

Feel the pain

It's not in vain

Let go of trivial things

Hear your liberty ring

Through your faith sing

For heaven sake don't believe the hype

Loving yourself should be more than a fling

Grasp and surrender discipline with
     consistency, even when it seems
     impossible to achieve

It is time now to resurrect your dream

Go against the stream

Dare to be caring and wise

Live for truth

Be fearless and courageous

      in the very midst of darkness

Seek the light that illuminates

      through your soul

Love from a healed, whole perspective

      becoming indeed your own, for that is

      the miracle in every moment

Life makes more sense when you don't have
      all the understanding you thought you
      needed

Become empowered to endure your storms
      by surrendering to the Way, the Truth,
      and the Light

A LOVE SO TRUE

I have a love so true

I don't mind sharing him with you

Never could I dream up a love that is so
      divine, too wonderful to just be called
      mine

He is not the kind of Lover you can put on a
      shelf, can't keep a love so sweet all to
      myself

So, if you're looking for a positive direction

      I recommend His affections

Don't be alarmed by His dominant ways
      just surrender to what He says
      yes, do whatever He says

You will never know a gentler touch or a
      heart so tender so true and thus I
      rarely feel blue because into His love I
      now surrender

I'm now in this moment, brand new, just
      wanting the world to feel the way I do
      so happy and peaceful too
      which is why I must share my love
      with you

Jesus, I have no words to describe how
      deeply your love has redirected my life
      I pray for your mercy and grace to be
      the woman of God You called me to be

Order and protect my steps

    let my spiritual wisdom discern the truth at all times

Give me an obedient heart

    help me to see when I'm getting off course and redirect me with Your gracious merciful love

No Judgement Self-Reflection Zone

_____
_____
_____
_____
_____
_____
_____
_____
_____
_____
_____
_____
_____
_____

JUST BE

Just be yourself

Just respect and learn to admire your
      uniqueness and all the imperfections
      you feel have been affecting your
      purpose and God-ordained destiny

Just live

      without fear

      always realize God is near

You are His

      under His divine protection

      He will keep you in the right direction

      depending on your heart's motive and affection

Just pray

> and avoid people, places, and things that have played their part in your life

Learn

> to love the pain as a lesson, the rejection as your protection

Just run

> from lust of every kind

> keep sharp, your spirit in tune and aligned to the will and still small voice of the Divine

Yes

> this world will try to wear you down

> don't let it

Just fight

> with integrity, wisdom, and love

Just seek

> the peace in the middle of chaos and
> lies

Just be wise

> without self-righteousness or pride
> and humble yourself

Be grateful

> that God is just and more than enough
> to help us in a trial

Just hold on

> endure and smile

Just let go

> of the self-hate, stop ruminating on
> the past

Just breath

    you're here now, in the moment

    in His presence

So just worship

    be content with His timing, trust in His word and study to live in the kingdom, on this earthly plane

Just trust

    in His timing, His will, His purpose for the storms and battles He allowed

Be grateful you survived

    get uncomfortable with just trying to escape and survive

Be determined

    to thrive and grow to help someone

        else to

            just be great

                and JUST BE

FAREWELL PARTY

The Real Turn Up

    I'm having a farewell party

    for some old friends

    They're leaving my life

    They no longer fit

    Well, you see, we all must admit

    and depart sometimes in our life

        in order to move on, so, goodbye to

        Loneliness, we've had our times, but

        now Faith and Love are here to keep

        me company

Farewell to Hurt, Anger, and Frustration
      which have always drained my energy

Fear, just walk out the door
      along with Pain and Jealousy
      taking Stress swiftly, along with Misery

You see, I took a stroll to seek what life was
      all about, so see ya my old dear friend
      and with this I speak to Doubt

I'll continue to stroll on as my new friends
      gather by my side – Love, Faith, Hope,
      and Confidence who've introduced me
      to their friends Peace of Mind,
      Happiness, and Positivity

Yes, my new friends truly bring out my best
	qualities, giving me room to grow and
	desiring the best for me

God redefined the word "friendship", can't
	you see? Now I desire to spend His
	time keeping productive company

It ignites the inner flame of my creativity, so
	I can share the stories of how
	wonderful life can be when we
	embrace love and let go of negativity

HEAVEN ON EARTH

The day goes quicker, you will see, when
    wonder ceases to be

No longer worried about the how or when

With each moment make a friend

Thoughts in dreams or love are the force
    that drives us to be

So, say a prayer to whom you cherish and let
    despair within you perish

If the truth is what you seek, work hard and
    the fact will come to its peak

Open up the heart within your soul so that
    you may unite an indeed be whole

The answer is not that far away

It lives within us each night and day

The choices you make create change to the life you want rearranged

So, embrace life by living and remember to share all the wisdom and riches that are now there

With these new actions you will find that heaven on Earth is peace of mind

No Judgement Self-Reflection Zone

_____
_____
_____
_____
_____
_____
_____
_____
_____
_____
_____
_____
_____

I KNOW WHAT IT'S LIKE

Pt.1

    I know what it's like to have your innocence stolen way too soon

    It's like total darkness

        no stars

        nor moon

    I know what it's like to be abandoned by the man who helped create me, never thinking to come by, call, or even take me

I know what it's like to feel victimized as a
      child by other children you want to
      befriend, yet they display hateful
      actions and tease you for no apparent
      reason

The loneliness a fragile heart goes through
      is such a delicate, rocky, and stormy
      season

I know what it feels like after all the
      emotional pain and turbulent times to
      dare and believe in love again

You open up your heart to people because
      you need to feel appreciated and
      protected, then betrayals take place
      and all you feel is neglected

            disrespected

                  and rejected

I know what it feels like to feel
>   misunderstood by someone you gave
>   your whole heart to and have it ripped
>   apart with suspicions and accusations
>   that are all lies

Yet, you still try to be submissive to them
>   and kind, praying that God will change
>   the situation so true love can shine

I know what it feels like to be talked down
>   to, degraded and told you are nothing
>   so many times that you start to feel
>   that way inside, to be hit so hard you
>   feel despised for just existing, and to
>   get hit harder because you appear to
>   be resisting

Hoping against hope that if you love them and be a better person, they'll see the real you and change, to be more loving, gentle, caring, and understanding instead of being lustful, distrustful, abusive, disloyal, and demanding

After all that I have been through I thank God now, through and through, because if not for these situations I could not have helped someone else's devastations

AS IF LONELINESS WERE MY FRIEND

As if Loneliness were my friend, we sit and talk about dreams and hopes of the past

As if Loneliness were my friend, he's always there to remind me just how foolish trying was

As if Loneliness were my friend, he sneaks up to catch me by surprise when happy times try to come

Yet, if Loneliness were truly my friend,
> Loneliness would love me enough to
> let me go

A GIFT TO MYSELF

I can feel the presence of a higher purpose
    leading me to and away from false
    ideas

I am flying like an eagle on a journey in my
    soul, I am growing like a naïve child
    yet so bold

I'm embracing all I don't know with the
    determination to learn, I am living out
    my desires as I dream for what I yearn

I'm letting go and receiving from myself
    what no one else can give, jumping
    into the emptiness to find the things
    one cannot see

I'm having faith in love when it seems to
    bring despair, I am embracing
    heartache to find joy in its touch

I am leaving behind all I knew and loved so
    much, off on an unknown journey into
    darkness so I can find the light within,
    forgiving all of me to begin again

I am building a solid foundation for each
    illusion that I find, strengthening my
    character, empowering my peace of
    mind

By being true to my moments each day, each
    minute, and each second in time,
    opening my heart to a love I always
    knew could be mine

I'm giving the gift of honor, respect, and
    dignity to myself as I let go of me and
    finally set myself free

No Judgement Self-Reflection Zone

_____
_____
_____
_____
_____
_____
_____
_____
_____
_____
_____
_____
_____
_____

GOOD HEART

My heart has been broken many times
>I've cried many tears from my past
lives, living in a constant battle,
choosing right from wrong

Men who pursued me lusted for my body
>tried to dominate or break my spirit
but no one cared if I genuinely had a
good heart

Trying to keep faith in my heart with good
>intentions, yet it is so hard to do alone

I would cherish a love that would be true to
    me, even if it's just a friend that
    knows how to appreciate my kind
    heart

I do need to care for someone with my
    whole heart, love without limitations
    to go beyond the superficial emotions
    no struggles or demands, yet sharing
    with compassion for one another's
    soul

At present, I explore my earlier mindset
    before I knew Christ as my Saviour
    I have to thank Him for being all I
    need so I can share my whole heart
    with Him

His love is absolute and He will never leave
    me, nor forsake me, thank you Lord
    Thank You

CLARITY

A moment in time when the knowledge in
      you knows the steps you must take to
      rise above what appears to be

feelings and emotions of hope and fear
      life and death in a breath

appreciating the magnificence
      in simplicity and in complexity

humanity that fosters joy and pain

I choose to rejoice that we are now aware
      that the process is necessary

and to try to take a shortcut diminishes the
      value of the impossible dream of peace
      in a world that promotes everything
      but...

LOVE WORTHY

No matter what happens or goes down
      I know I'm worthy of being loved now

I've been loved by the best, been put to so
      many tests, hung on and let go, gave
      love away because my foolish heart
      said so

I'm no angel and I've been a fool, broken
      hearts and relationship rules
      inside I had to rise to find the real me
      so I could genuinely love myself
      unconditionally

Lessons learned and experiences earned
> showed me ups and downs, but I know
> I'm worthy to love and truly be loved
> now

I MOVE ON

I never have to stay to play a role in
> somebody's life that's not positive and
> bright, for if you can't feed my light
> goodnight

> > I'm out of sight

> > I move on

Sometimes I stumble onto many doorways
> that are not meant for me to see or be

> > So, I move on

I don't stick around to be tolerated by few
> when I can be celebrated by God,

family, and real friends, for in my soul I am rich, I have plenty to spare but if you're not a part of the plan God has for me

    I move on

I don't sit around complaining, blaming about the injustice that was done to me or mine, I live in the now moment so God's love helps me shine, to learn to get wiser while

    I move on

I no longer hang out with sadness and depression, I give it to God to handle it, and guess what

    I move on

My heart is open to the sweet sounds of life so long struggle, stress, and strife if you and I can't build something positive and right I'm through

I move on

So, if all you bring to the table is spoiled food for thought, I'm not hungry for drama because

I've moved on.

No Judgement Self-Reflection Zone

_____
_____
_____
_____
_____
_____
_____
_____
_____
_____
_____
_____
_____
_____

MY LONELINESS

My loneliness is not a sad cry

I wish for many to hear

For me it is a celebration of my soul

Which chooses on her own to strive to be the best in God, business, family, and friendship

My loneliness is a parade of greatness

guiding me through the darkness of insecurities, for I am but a soldier fighting an inner war to be as honest with myself as to this mission of life

My loneliness and I are faithful to one
      another, we talk, we laugh, we cry,
      and we watch together, witnessing
      relationships of friends

My loneliness and I move on smoothly as
      the music plays a harmonious tune for
      me to dance in joy, in peace, and in
      love despite betrayals

Sometimes, my loneliness and I spend our
      time looking into sorrow's eyes,
         finding the peace in our own existence

SOBER MIND

My eyes are now open wide as well as my
>mind

I'm free to fly above a dark emptiness
>for
>>I have found a sober mind

I no longer hang with doubt

I move along to create, to grow, and to
>branch out
>>for
>>>I have found a sober mind

I'm becoming smarter with the
      acknowledgment of things I don't
      know, yes in this world I have grown

    for

            I have found a sober mind

The world within is clean and pure, I'm
      feeling more secure

    for

            I have found a sober mind

It arrived right on time, has me singing in
      rhymes, I am no longer blind,
      laughing at fear and worry free

    for

            I have found a sober mind

ORIGIN OF WISDOM

Where does wisdom come from

whispered my youthful soul

It comes from everything made in this world

    God ordained it

        His gift to those who will follow

        wisdom regardless of what they

        desire, for it is the integral,

        purposeful, divine holy fire

It can come from joy

It may come from gain, pain, or loss

It may appear in the day or arrive at night

Wisdom never sleeps

It's always on its job

It dwells within our dreams and guards our foolish heart if we take heed to its insight

It's in our mind to guard our souls as we trust in the unknown process of becoming new, abiding in the peace, truth, and honor wisdom brings

ACTION SPEAKS

Action speaks to the universe, the Creator
He hears our prayers and knows we
are sincere through action

Actions speak to loved ones no matter what
is said, so make a kind gesture of love
before you go to bed

Action will speak to them, and while they
are sleep, love will grow wider,
stronger and help you find real
friends, for words don't mean a thing
unless you put action on the scene

THE TRUTH

When you are true to you, there is nothing
      you can't do

When you stand your ground, nothing or
      nobody will ever keep you down

If you believe and take a chance, you'll bring
      to life a dream with your deeds

Every burning need will be fulfilled without
      doubt or fear

And from inside of you the truth will be
      revealed

No Judgement Self-Reflection Zone

About the Author

Lady Tiffany was born and raised in the Bronx, New York. She started early in the entertainment field, singing background vocals for Rhonda Ross, daughter of the legendary Diana Ross, a partnership acquired through her tight-knit community of friends which included the late, Grammy-award winner, Edwin Birdsong.

Lady Tiffany is an artist at heart, aided by her personal essence expressed in her numerous poems, songs, and inspirational words which continue to touch lives. In addition to singing and writing, Lady Tiffany is an enthusiastic cook, homeopathic lifestyle coach, devoted mother, and loyal friend.

Made in the USA
Middletown, DE
11 December 2019